UNITED STATES BY REGION

People and Places of the
SOUTHWEST

by Danielle Smith-Llera

Consultant:
Dr. David Lanegran
John S. Holl Professor of Geography
Macalester College
St. Paul, Minnesota

CAPSTONE PRESS
a capstone imprint

Fact Finders Books are published by Capstone Press,
1710 Roe Crest Drive, North Mankato, Minnesota 56003
www.mycapstone.com

Copyright © 2017 by Capstone Press, a Capstone imprint. All rights reserved. No part of this publication may be reproduced in whole or in part, or stored in a retrieval system, or transmitted in any form or by any means, electronic, mechanical, photocopying, recording, or otherwise, without written permission of the publisher.

Library of Congress Cataloging-in-Publication Data
Names: Smith-Llera, Danielle, 1971- author.
Title: People and places of the Southwest / by Danielle Smith-Llera.
Description: North Mankato, Minnesota : Fact Finders Books, an imprint of
  Capstone Press, 2017. | Series: Fact finders. United States by region |
  Includes bibliographical references and index.
Identifiers: LCCN 2016010777| ISBN 9781515724421 (library binding) | ISBN
  9781515724476 (pbk.) | ISBN 9781515724520 (ebook pdf)
Subjects: LCSH: Southwest, New—Juvenile literature.
Classification: LCC F785.7 .S65 2017 | DDC 979—dc23
LC record available at http://lccn.loc.gov/2016010777

Editorial Credits
Angie Kaelberer, editor; Cynthia Della-Rovere, designer; Svetlana Zhurkin, media researcher; Laura Manthe, production specialist

Photo Credits
Alamy: A.T. Willett, 16–17, Curt Wiler, cover (top); Getty Images: Ed Vebell, 12, Tony Vaccaro, 29; iStockphoto: Lokibaho, 26–27; NASA, 23; Newscom: Picture History, 10; North Wind Picture Archives, 11; Shutterstock: aceshot1, 28, Everett Historical, 13, FeyginFoto, 14–15, holbox, cover (bottom), IrinaK, 18, Jim Parkin, 21, jorik, 19, Leigh Anne Meeks, 25, Martin M303, 6–7, Tim Roberts Photography, 9

Design and Map Elements by Shutterstock

Table of Contents

Introduction 4

Chapter 1: History and Growth 8

Chapter 2: Land and Climate 14

Chapter 3: Jobs and Economy 20

Chapter 4: People and Culture 24

Glossary *30*

Read More *31*

Internet Sites *31*

Index *32*

Introduction

Bright blue skies and sunshine happen here nearly every day. Mountains rise over flat deserts and grassland. And deep rivers flow through colorful canyons. Where can you find all of this beauty? It can all be found in the Southwest region of the United States.

The Southwest includes only four states. They are Oklahoma, Arizona, Texas, and New Mexico. But the region is not small. All of its states are large in area. Texas is the second largest state after Alaska.

The region's population is large as well. Texas is second only to California in population. The other three states rank in the middle. The region's cities are among the fastest growing in the United States. Many people move there for the warm weather and year-round outdoor activities.

The Southwest Region by Rank

Let's see how the states in the Southwest region compare to each other. This chart includes each state in the Southwest and ranks it by population and area. Also included are each state's capital and nickname. It's easy to understand why Arizona is called the Grand Canyon State. But why do you think Oklahoma's nickname is the Sooner State? You might have to do a little research to learn that reason!

The famous canyon in Arizona helped the state earn the nickname the Grand Canyon State.

State	Population	Rank	Square Miles	Rank	Capital	Nickname
Arizona	6,731,484	15	114,006	6	Phoenix	Grand Canyon State
New Mexico	2,085,572	36	121,598	5	Santa Fe	Land of Enchantment
Oklahoma	3,878,051	28	69,903	20	Oklahoma City	Sooner State
Texas	26,956,958	2	268,601	2	Austin	Lone Star State

Chapter 1
History and Growth

For more than 10,000 years, people have lived in the Southwest. The first people who lived there were ancestors of the Apache, Navajo, Hopi, Comanche, and Pueblo American Indians. The hot, dry climate was a challenge, but they learned to use nature to survive.

American Indians built **adobe** homes with many rooms and floors by covering wood and stone with clay. People sometimes built these flat-topped houses inside caves. The cave walls kept them cool and safe from enemies.

FACT

During World War II, Navajo "code talkers" helped the United States and its allies send radio messages. Their complex language was a code enemy countries could not break.

adobe: bricks made of clay and straw that are dried in the sun

The Indians planted sunflowers, squash, beans, and corn. They found ways to farm even if the land wasn't flat. They cut steps into hillsides or planted on the flat tops of **mesas**. They dug ditches from rivers to water the crops.

Long ago American Indians built this cliff dwelling in Canyon De Chelly, Arizona.

mesa: a broad hill with a flat top and steep sides

American Indians in Oklahoma

Oklahoma has a rich American Indian heritage. Before it became a state, part of it was called Indian Territory. Several tribes are native to the state, including the Kiowa, Osage, Wichita, and Caddo. But some came to the state by force. In the early 1800s, white settlers in the Southeast wanted American Indian lands. These lands belonged to Cherokees, Creeks, Choctaws, Chickasaws, and Seminoles. In 1830 the Indian Removal Act ordered tribe members to give up their land. They had to move to **reservations** in Indian Territory.

Some tribes moved while others fought to stay where they were. The Choctaw and Chickasaw saw no other choice and agreed to move. The Seminoles moved after fighting several wars with the U.S. Army. The Creek moved after threats from the army. But the Cherokee held out. In 1837 President Andrew Jackson got the army involved. Soldiers forced more than 16,000 Cherokee to walk 1,000 miles (1,609 kilometers) west. About 4,000 people died from disease, hunger, and cold on the four-month journey. It became known as the Trail of Tears. Today the five tribes live on Oklahoma reservations.

reservation: an area of land set aside by the U.S. government for American Indians

Spanish Explorers

Spanish explorers were the first Europeans to settle in the Southwest. They arrived in Mexico in 1517 and made it a Spanish colony. In 1540 the explorers traveled north into present-day Arizona and New Mexico. By 1600 Spanish settlers and priests arrived in the area. They established farms and built churches. Spanish soldiers protected these **missions**.

Spanish missions had an important role in creating what is now the Southwest region of the United States.

The Spanish wanted the Pueblo Indians to follow the Christian religion. The settlers forced them to work in the missions and often punished them. Pueblo Indians from more than 70 villages took up weapons in 1680. They pushed the Spanish out of the area for more than 10 years.

Much later, the Spanish were pushed out of the region for good. Mexican colonists fought a war against Spain and won independence in 1821. Mexico took control of the land, missions, and people of the Southwest.

mission: a church or settlement where religious leaders live and work

11

Under Mexican Rule

Many French settlers lived in Louisiana, which bordered the Mexican region of Texas. Mexico worried that American Indians and French settlers would gain control of Texas. Mexico offered Texas land to people from outside its borders. Many American settlers moved to Texas. However, they didn't want to live under Mexican rule.

These settlers started the Texas Revolution against Mexico in 1835. In March 1836 Mexican soldiers defeated them in a battle at the Alamo mission in San Antonio. This defeat made the settlers fight harder. They won independence for Texas a month later. In 1845 Texas became a U.S. state.

The United States and Mexico continued to argue over the border between their countries. Mexican soldiers attacked American soldiers and started the Mexican-American War in 1846. The United States won the war in 1848 and got Mexican land. This included most of present-day Arizona and New Mexico.

American settlers in Texas were defeated by Mexican soldiers during the Battle of the Alamo.

Homesteading

In 1803 President Thomas Jefferson bought a huge area of land from France in the Louisiana Purchase. It included present-day Oklahoma. U.S. leaders wanted Americans to settle its new lands. In 1862 President Abraham Lincoln signed the Homestead Act. The government promised free land to anyone who would settle and farm it for five years.

Southwestern settlers survived great challenges. In the 1920s and 1930s, **droughts** dried up farmland in Great **Plains** states, including Oklahoma, Texas, and New Mexico. People called the area the Dust Bowl.

Big dust storms hit parts of the Southwest during the 1930s. The storms were caused by drought and lack of good farming methods.

drought: a long period of weather with little or no rainfall

plains: a large, flat area of land with few trees

FACT

In 1889 the government offered land in Oklahoma. People waited excitedly for a military officer to shoot a pistol and start the race to claim land. Because hundreds of people slipped in early to claim land, Oklahoma's nickname became the Sooner State.

Chapter 2
Land and Climate

The Southwest is a dry region. The Sierra Nevada Mountains in California block moisture from the Pacific Ocean. Deserts in New Mexico and Arizona may get less than 10 inches (25 centimeters) of rainfall each year. Temperatures that are more than 100 degrees Fahrenheit (38 degrees Celsius) can bake the soil until it cracks. But the region is full of life. Thick grasses wave across the plains of central Texas and Oklahoma. In the desert, cacti tower up to 60 feet (18 meters). Joshua trees can live hundreds of years.

The Southwest has little coastline. The Gulf of Mexico borders southeastern Texas. Several major rivers and lakes provide water for the region. The Rio Grande flows from Colorado through central New Mexico. It forms the border between Texas and Mexico before emptying into the Gulf of Mexico. The Colorado River formed the Grand Canyon in Arizona. The river provides water for people in such cities as Phoenix and Tucson, Arizona. The Hoover Dam forms Lake Mead on the Colorado River between Nevada and Arizona.

The Hoover Dam is between Arizona and Nevada. It was built to bring water and power to the Southwest.

Weather

The region is often called the "sunny Southwest." Phoenix, Arizona, has more than 300 days of sunshine. New Mexico is also known for its dry weather, clear skies, and colorful sunsets. Texas includes dry areas in the west but wetter areas on the Gulf Coast. These places receive more than 60 inches (152 cm) of rain. In Oklahoma, rainfall ranges between 17 inches (43 cm) in the west to 56 inches (142 cm) in the east.

Along with sunshine, the region experiences major storms. **Tornadoes** tear across the flat land of Oklahoma and Texas. **Hurricanes** sometimes hit the Gulf Coast region of Texas. The deadliest U.S. hurricane hit the city of Galveston in 1900. It killed at least 6,000 people. Huge dust storms called haboobs sometimes fill Arizona's skies.

Tornadoes often happen in parts of the Southwest. This one was photographed in Texas.

tornado: a spinning column of air that looks like a funnel

hurricane: a very large storm with rain and high winds

Natural Wonders and Wildlife

Visitors to New Mexico can explore the Carlsbad Caverns. The caverns contain more than 100 bat-filled caves deep in the Chihuahuan Desert. The desert is also home to the White Sands National Monument. Visitors can sled down the sand dunes. In Arizona's Petrified Forest National Park, glittering trees were buried in rock for 200 million years.

FACT

The most western area of Oklahoma is called the Panhandle because it is shaped like a frying pan.

People enjoy sledding down sand dunes at White Sands National Monument in New Mexico.

The Grand Canyon

About 5 million years ago, the Colorado River began shaping the Grand Canyon in Arizona. The river slowly wore away the soil and revealed colorful rock layers. The canyon is more than 1 mile (1.6 km) deep and as much as 18 miles (29 km) wide.

Each year nearly 5 million people visit the canyon. Some hike or ride mules into the canyon bottom. Once there they can travel by raft on the river.

People can also see deep into the canyon from above. The Hualapai Indians have built a skywalk on their tribal land. The horseshoe-shaped glass platform stretches about 70 feet (21 m) from the canyon's edge.

The Southwest is also home to many animals. They include large lizards, such as the Gila monster, and poisonous snakes, such as western diamondback and sidewinder rattlesnakes. Scorpions and tarantulas burrow in the desert sand. The armadillo is so common in Texas that it's been named the state animal. The armadillo's body is covered with bony plates that help protect it.

Chapter 3
Jobs and Economy

Today, glass skyscrapers rise from modern southwestern cities. Busy people drive on multilane highways. In rural areas and small towns, people work in a variety of industries.

Ranching

Beef and dairy products bring billions of dollars into the Southwest. Texas is the nation's top beef producer.

Spanish settlers first brought cows and sheep. Beginning in the 1850s, Texas cowhands herded cattle north on the Abilene Trail to railroad stations in Kansas. From there the cattle were transported all over the country. Today about 12 million cattle live on Texas ranches.

Farming

Farmers in the Southwest grow food year-round. However, the lack of rainfall can be a problem. Farmers **irrigate** their crops with sprinklers or pipes. Much of the lettuce, broccoli, cauliflower, and spinach Americans eat grow in Arizona's Yuma Valley. In Texas, the Rio Grande provides water for fields and orchards.

Texas is by far the largest cotton producer in the United States. Oklahoma and Arizona farmers also grow cotton. A type of cotton called pima was named for the Pima Indian tribe. This soft, strong cotton is used to make clothing and bedding.

Lots of sunshine and good soil make Yuma Valley a great spot for growing vegetables. It is actually the nation's third largest vegetable producer!

irrigate: to supply water for crops using channels or pipes

Black Gold

Spanish settlers hoped to find gold in the Southwest. But a greater treasure lay under the ground. It was huge pools of oil. American Indians found oil hundreds of years ago in Texas and Oklahoma. By the early 1900s wells pumped the oil from beneath the ground. People hoping to get rich rushed to the region. Towns near the oil fields boomed. Oil helped develop major southwestern cities. They included Tulsa and Oklahoma City in Oklahoma, and Dallas, Houston, and Fort Worth in Texas. Oil companies still bring hundreds of billions of dollars to the region.

Research and Technology

The region attracts highly skilled workers. During World War II (1939–1945), scientists built a secret laboratory in Los Alamos, New Mexico. Open spaces with few people allowed them to test the first nuclear bombs. Today engineers still work on weapons and defense systems in cities such as Tucson.

The National Aeronautic and Space Administration (NASA) tests rockets in Las Cruces, New Mexico. Aerospace engineers work at NASA's Johnson Space Center in Houston, Texas. From there flight controllers guided the first moon landing in 1969. Today the center trains astronauts.

The teams that work at the Johnson Space Center's Mission Control have watched over activities in space since 1965.

Chapter 4
People and Culture

The Southwest has a mixture of cultures. Latinos make up a large part of the populations of Texas, New Mexico, and Arizona. They form 47 percent of New Mexico's population. More American Indians live in the Southwest than any other U.S. region. Oklahoma has the second-largest American Indian population. It's second only to California.

Food

Like American Indians, southwestern cooks depend on corn and beans. They fold corn tortillas around beans, meat, vegetables, and even eggs. They stuff corn husks with meat to make tamales.

Southwestern cooks also rely on the flavors of Spanish cooking. Spanish explorers brought onions and garlic. Chile peppers came from Mexico. Cooks add spice to dishes with these peppers.

Barbecue dishes are popular too because of the area's rich ranching history. Cooks smoke meat using oak, pecan, or mesquite wood from local trees.

Tex-Mex dishes combine flavors from Texas and Mexico. These tacos filled with eggs are a popular Tex-Mex dish.

Outdoor Fun

Parks bring nature inside cities. In downtown Oklahoma City, the Prairie Garden has many grasses and flowers of the prairie. In Tucson, about 400,000 people visit the Arizona-Sonora Desert Museum each year. They walk paths through plants, fish tanks, and displays of minerals.

Many southwestern cities encourage residents to enjoy biking throughout the year. Houston has more than 300 miles (483 km) of bike paths. San Antonio bikers can check out a bicycle from a station and drop it off at another. Paved bike paths in Albuquerque, New Mexico, lead out of the city into the mountains.

FACT

Each spring, people gather at the Albuquerque International Balloon Fiesta. They watch 500 colorful hot air balloons rise against the blue sky and Sandia Mountains.

These bikers ride on trails near Sedona, Arizona.

Arts and Culture

Santa Fe, New Mexico, is known worldwide as an art center. Its galleries and museums draw more than 1 million visitors each year. At the Indian Market in Santa Fe, artists from more than 100 tribes sell works made of clay, silver, and leather.

Throughout the year, southwesterners celebrate their history. American Indians hold powwows. They dress in traditional clothing and perform ancient dances. Each April thousands of people come to Albuquerque's Old Town for a fiesta. American Indian drummers beat rhythms for dancers in buffalo skins. Musicians play Mexican mariachi music on guitars, violins, and trumpets.

Thousands of American Indian dancers and singers come to the Gathering of Nations Powwow in Albuquerque, New Mexico.

The Southwest is a land of stark but stunning landscapes. This rugged beauty continues to inspire people who live in the region. Each of their lives adds to its rich history.

Georgia O'Keeffe

Artist Georgia O'Keeffe was born in Wisconsin in 1887. She studied art in both Chicago and New York. She first traveled to northern New Mexico in 1929. The desert landscape inspired her richly colored paintings and drawings of rocks, plants, bones, and skies. O'Keeffe moved to New Mexico in 1949. She continued creating her huge desert paintings well into her 80s. She died in Santa Fe in 1986 at age 98. Today the Georgia O'Keeffe Museum in Santa Fe holds thousands of her works.

Glossary

adobe (uh-DOH-bee)—bricks made of clay and straw that are dried in the sun

drought (DROUT)—a long period of weather with little or no rainfall

hurricane (HUR-uh-kane)—a very large storm with rain and high winds

irrigate (IHR-uh-gate)—to supply water for crops using channels or pipes

mesa (MAY-suh)—a broad hill with a flat top and steep sides

mission (MISH-uhn)—a church or settlement where religious leaders live and work

plains (PLAYNZ)—a large, flat area of land with few trees

reservation (rez-er-VAY-shuhn)—an area of land set aside by the U.S. government for American Indians

tornado (tor-NAY-doh)—a spinning column of air that looks like a funnel

Read More

Bartley, Niccole. *The Southwest.* Land that I Love. New York: PowerKids Press, 2015.

Krasner, Barbara. *Native Nations of the Southwest.* Native Nations of North America. Mankato, Minn.: Child's World, 2015.

Owens, L. L. *Southwestern Region.* United States Regions. Vero Beach, Fla.: Rourke Educational Media, 2016.

Peppas, Lynn. *What's in the Southwest?* All around the U.S. New York: Crabtree Publishing Company, 2012.

Internet Sites

FactHound offers a safe, fun way to find Internet sites related to this book. All of the sites on FactHound have been researched by our staff.

Here's all you do:

Visit www.facthound.com

Type in this code: 9781515724421

Check out projects, games and lots more at
www.capstonekids.com

Index

American Indians, 8–9, 10, 11, 12, 22, 24, 28
  Trail of Tears, 10

animals, 19

art, 28, 29

Carlsbad Caverns, 18

cities, 5, 15, 20, 22, 26
  Albuquerque, 26, 28
  Dallas, 22
  Oklahoma City, 7, 22, 26
  Phoenix, 7, 15, 16
  Santa Fe, 7, 28, 29

Dust Bowl, 13

farms, 9, 11, 13, 21

food, 21, 24

Grand Canyon, 6, 15, 19

Hoover Dam, 15

lakes, 15

land, 4, 9, 10, 11, 12, 13, 17, 19, 29
  deserts, 4, 14
  Great Plains, 13

Mexican-American War, 12

missions, 11

museums, 26, 28, 29

music, 28

oil, 22

O'Keeffe, Georgia, 29

plants, 26, 29

population, 5, 6, 7, 24

rain, 14, 16, 21

rivers, 4, 9, 15

storms, 17

temperatures, 14

Texas Revolution, 12

White Sands National Monument, 18

work, 11, 20, 22, 23